Presented to

_____

With Love From

_____

Date

_____

The Christmas Shoes

& other heart-warming stories

Leonard Ahlstrom

The Christmas Shoes
© 2001 by Leonard Ahlstrom
All rights reserved. Printed in the United States of America.
Published by Point to Point, Old Hickory, Tennessee 37138.

"The Christmas Shoes" written by Leonard Ahlstrom and Eddie Carswell.
© 2000 Warner/Chappell, Smith Haven's Music (ASCAP)/Sony ATV (BMI).
All rights reserved. No portion of this publication may be reproduced in any form without the prior written permission of the publisher except in the case of brief quotations within critical articles and reviews.

Unless otherwise indicated, all Scripture quotations in this book are from the New American Standard (NAS) Open Bible, © 1985 Thomas Nelson, Inc., Publishers.

Distributed in partnership with Premium Press America.
For information call 1-800-891-7323.
Graphic Design—Bill Collier
Photography—Melissa McCallister
Editors—Shirleen Louviere and Rebecca L. Ahlstrom

ISBN: 0-9714147-0-X
Printed and bound in the United States of America.

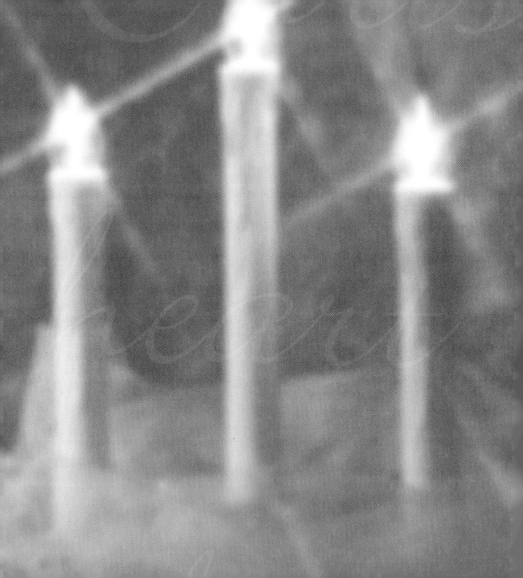

"I will honor Christmas
in my heart
and try to keep it
all year."

Charles Dickens

About the Song—

Songs are amazing. They can touch the heart in ways that nothing else can. As co-writer and producer of "The Christmas Shoes," I knew it was a special song, but had had no idea of the impact that it would have on others.

Two years ago, I received a copy of an internet story titled "True Christmas Spirit" that D.C. Chymes, co-host of the syndicated *Steve & D.C. in the Morning* radio show in St. Louis, would read on the air during the holidays. "Every time that I have read the story, the phone lines have gone crazy," he said. "I think it's a great idea for a song."

D.C. was right. It was inspiration for a wonderful song but such a challenge to write—as many heart-breaking stories are. The internet story of the little boy haunted my co-writer Eddie Carswell and I for months. After many failed attempts and even giving up a couple of times, finally we felt that we had captured the story's emotion in song.

John Mays, President of Benson Records, asked me to produce the song. Without hesitation I said, "Yes." He then informed me that I had only seven days to complete production if it were to be included on the NewSong recording project. That, however, wasn't the real challenge. Four of those seven days I was to be on the road with NewSong, playing guitar—which left only three days to record, mix and master the song.

Everything fell completely in to place as if orchestrated from heaven. It wasn't until later that I realized the miracle that had taken place. And all I had to do to see it, to experience it, was simply say, "Yes."

8

Apparently "The Christmas Shoes" song struck a chord with radio listeners as it became the #1 song on the Billboard AC chart the week of Christmas 2000. Since then I have received a flood of stories as a result of hearing the song. This book contains a few of those stories. I hope they remind you, as they did me, that Christmas begins in the heart.

"I stopped the busyness of my day,
stood still...listening,
tears falling, touched simply
by the unselfishness of a
young boy's love."

Zoe L. Robicheaux

The Christmas Shoes

by Leonard Ahlstrom & Eddie Carswell

It was almost Christmas time
There I stood in another line
Tryin' to buy that last gift or two
Not really in the Christmas mood

Standing right in front of me
Was a little boy waiting anxiously
Pacing round like little boys do
And in his hands he held a pair of shoes

And his clothes were worn and old
He was dirty from head to toe
And when it came his time to pay
I couldn't believe what I heard him say

(Chorus) "Sir, I want to buy these shoes
For my mama, please
It's Christmas Eve and these shoes are just her size
Could you hurry, Sir
Daddy says there's not much time
You see, she's been sick for quite awhile
And I know these shoes will make her smile
And I want her to look beautiful
If Mama meets Jesus tonight"

They counted pennies for what seemed like years
Then the cashier said, "Son, there's not enough here"
He searched his pockets frantically
Then he turned and he looked at me
He said, "Mama made Christmas good at our house
Though most years she just did without
Tell me, Sir, what am I gonna do
Somehow I've got to buy her these Christmas shoes"

So I laid the money down
I just had to help him out
I'll never forget the look on his face
When he said, "Mama's gonna look so great"

(Chorus) "Sir, I want to buy these shoes
For my mama, please
It's Christmas Eve and these shoes are just her size
Could you hurry, Sir
Daddy says there's not much time
You see, she's been sick for quite awhile
And I know these shoes will make her smile
And I want her to look beautiful
If Mama meets Jesus tonight"

(Bridge) I knew I caught a glimpse of heaven's love
As he thanked me and ran out
I knew that God had sent that little boy
To remind me what Christmas is all about

*"How wonderful it is
that nobody need wait
a single minute
before starting to improve
the world."*

Anne Frank

15

From the Author–

This book has been a bitter-sweet project for me. It brought back memories of my best Christmas and also my saddest.

Back in 1964, on a cold December Amarillo evening, there was a knock at our front door. I don't recall why *I* was the one who answered the door, but I was glad that I did. At that very moment my whole world changed.

Standing in front of me was my father who had been gone for a very long time. He was back. You see, there was a time when I—his only son—was his shadow, his buddy. It was hard to be a shadow to someone who wasn't around. But that day my dad came back!

Christmas was great that year. I had the best gift I could have ever hoped for—my dad and mom together again. Unfortunately, within the following months, my dad unexpectedly died in our home and some of my dreams died with him.

That next Christmas was the hardest Christmas for me. I was only eight.

Now, as a husband and father of three incredible children, my heart's desire is to give my family things I didn't have—a father's time and an abundance of great memories.

This book, although hard at times for me, has been a labor of love. I hope it will stir up fond memories for you and bring your heart warmth throughout this holiday season.

Leonard Ahlstrom

"The heart has its reasons
which reason does not
understand."

Blaise Pascal (1623–1662)

Christmas With Grampa

Christmas With Grampa

Caro Louviere

As an only child and a lonely child, Christmas was special to me. That was the time when families gathered.

My favorite gathering was the one with my father's parents, whose French ancestors had been exiled from Nova Scotia by the British in 1755. They had migrated to South Louisiana, settling on a land grant north of Lafayette. Because they were outcasts, these Acadians valued a closed and close-knit, highly structured family life. Evident was signs of their strong Catholic faith: morning prayers, the rosary, evening prayers and Mass. Religious pictures, a crucifix in every room, prayer cards, a large picture of a daughter in her nun's habit, and one of an "angel" young daughter that had died.

During World War II, nothing had changed. Schools still enforced "English only" classrooms, and the general climate was anti-French.

Christmas Eve in 1944 was a memorable one for me. Nine years of age, I was becoming aware of how important family time is. By early evening, everyone had arrived at the farm of Grampa Theodule and Gramma Agnes.

The three-bedroom cream-colored home was the only painted one in the area. That didn't mean that they were rich, but that my grandparents knew the value of keeping things owned in tip-top shape. The house had been built four feet off the ground in case of floods, and it was surrounded on three sides by porches. High ceilings kept rooms cool. The only luxury was piped-in water; other than that, no electricity, bathroom, etc.

While waiting for nightfall over twenty of us grandkids played tag and war games in the pecan grove. We shared our hopes of Santa's arrival. The adults shared crop failures, lack of money, rationing of metal and sugar, and war stories. Four uncles were overseas: two sailors, one soldier, and one marine.

By seven o'clock, the routine that I loved had begun. We had been herded inside, had been fed, hands and feet washed, and had gathered in front of the living room fireplace. There had never been a Christmas tree, but a meager little manger had a place of honor on the sideboard. And there was the picture of the "Last Supper" above the long plank-board table.

Grampa Theodule sat in his big overstuffed chair across the room and watched as each of us put our shoes in our chosen place. That is where, hopefully, Santa would put a gift—one each per child. I had kept my same lucky place each year. The year before I had received a flashlight for barn chores at night.

Babies were then shushed as everyone sat quietly and listened as each military wife translated in French her last letter from her husband. I saw tears and babies held closer to mommas, and I moved closer to Grampa. I heard his words of comfort and prayer that "all his boys" would be returned safely.

Grampa was my idol, and I was his shadow. The first time I had seen a picture of Abraham Lincoln in school, I had thought it was a picture of Grampa. In his seventies, he was very tall and thin, with kind brown eyes.

Soft-spoken, a listener who spoke in slow, carefully thought-out words, Grampa was respected and was sought out for advice by his children, neighbors, and me. He had never smoked and permitted no alcohol in his home. Those who chose to drink hid their liquor in cars or in the barn. Grampa never fussed, never argued, but all knew he was the head of the family.

As his oldest grandchild, I felt favored as I often sat with Grampa on one of the porches, drinking McCormick root beer or a cold glass of milk from a Mason jar that had been tied with a string and cooled in the cistern water.

By nine o'clock all of us kids had knelt together and recited, "The Lord's

21

Prayer." Added to this were our personal petitions, asking God to bless parents, siblings, pets, and to end the war.

Then Gramma Agnes helped mommas put the children down to sleep. Gramma was the exact opposite of Grampa and much younger. A tiny wisp of a woman, weighing less than ninety pounds, she never stopped. Rising at daylight, she and the daughters fed the animals, milked the cows, and returned to make breakfast before the men awakened. She was the last to go to bed.

Sometimes Gramma spoke to us in "broken-English," learned from her school-aged daughters. She was very patient, forgiving, and trusting. We kids fibbed, adults lied; yet she believed in our basic goodness, quickly excusing bad behavior with kind words, like "poor thing," "you tried very hard," "maybe your head hurt," "this heat (or cold) weather can make us do strange things," "he's not drunk; he's sick."

The only time I had ever seen her quiet was when she read her special French book of prayers, her blue eyes squinting to see the tiny words. Over her neat little bun, she always wore a French bonnet with the beak folded upward, and full-bodied apron over her dress. And she seldom sat "lady-like" on one of her many wooden rockers or cowhide-bottomed chairs; she curled one foot under her, the other foot dangling, not able to touch the floor.

Gramma's sleeping arrangement was six kids to a bed; others on folded quilts on the pine floors with wide cracks that let the cold wind whistle through.

From my vantage point and too excited to sleep, I watched the women in the living room, removing left-over pieces of pecan cake, nibbling as they did. I could hear the men in the kitchen laughing and commenting that once they returned from Midnight Mass, they would eat sandwiches of pork roast, one of five that Gramma had cooked in a cast iron pot over an open fire outdoors earlier that morning. (Every Catholic was expected to fast at least one hour before Mass.) And I kept a watchdog eye on my shoes, while listening for sleigh bells on the roof.

Sleep finally came and while we slept, the adults left for church in Lafayette six miles away. Two mommas stayed behind with us.

By two o'clock the churchgoers returned. Grampa sat in his stuffed armchair and then summoned parents to awaken us kids. He enjoyed watching us as we ran to our shoes. The other adults enjoyed watching Grampa as he called each of us by name to come to him to show the gift.

I happily showed him my green wooden machine gun that rat-a-tat-tatted. I told him that I had heard sleigh bells on the roof. Others laughed; he did not. Another kid came crying with disappointment, unhappy with her tea set instead of the stuffed doll she had wanted. He soothed her with caressing touch and gentle words, making her and her gift special.

The scene shifted to one of chaos mixed with glee: crying, laughter, cap guns firing, wooden train engine "choo-chooing" across the floor, momma quietly shussing an angry kid, and daddies rocking sleep-deprived babies. No kid grabbed another kid's gift. Each knew better.

The night came to an end as we gathered up wrapping paper and string and tossed them into the fire that crackled and changed colors. Meanwhile, Gramma oversaw the snack making for the kids: cane syrup and butter on homemade bread and a cup of milk. Then it was bedtime again.

Grampa Theodule died when I was fourteen, and Gramma Agnes, a few years ago. The memory of that special time is often in my thoughts now that I am a grandfather. My recollection has never changed. For even though some grandchildren went to bed disappointed with their gifts that night, all felt the snuggling warmth of a family's love. Isn't that the greatest gift of all?

"You will find,

as you look back upon your life,

that the moments that stand out

are the moments when you

have done things for others."

Henry Drummond

A Fish Story

A Fish Story

Rick Cua

(An Italian Christmas)

My story is about fish. . .all kinds of fish, Smelt, Bacala (Cod), Calamari, Eel, Clams, Mussels, Octopus. Many things that swim and a few things that crawl. That would be Christmas Eve at my house. Without a doubt, a beautiful gift, a sign of love and one heck of a meal!

My earliest memory of this blessed yearly event was watching my mom, grandmothers, aunts and assorted other female relatives working in the kitchen making sure everything was perfect. It was like a culinary university of sorts. The older women teaching the younger women and every one teaching the kids. Of course it would have been quicker for the experienced to just do it themselves but that thought never crossed their minds. After all, they knew there was more to life than just convenience.

A few of the older women had physical problems yet they would stay on their feet all day long. I can still see them bent over a wooden board on the kitchen table rolling out dough, cutting homemade pasta, and preparing the fish in a variety of ways. It wasn't good enough, for example, to just have calamari breaded and fried. We had it in the sauce, stuffed, sauteed scampi style, in a cold salad, etc. And, it was the same for many of the different fish. Truly a labor of love, and for those of us who were fortunate enough to participate in this Italian Christmas Eve feast—a religious experience!

I remember, as they cooked, they would talk to each other—family things, personal things, laughing and crying at times, too. They gave us and each other what they could give—the gift of themselves wrapped in a great meal. An offering to the Lord through serving the people He and they loved. Just for the record, this didn't only happen at Christmas, it happened year round. Not the fish—although most of my relatives did grow up surrounded by water on three sides—but this wonderful gift.

Actually, as I look back I realize that what they really gave us was their time. Unselfishly, never withholding it and to all. So what's my story really about? It's about loving people by giving them one of your most valued assets—your time.

At Christmas and everyday of the year take time for God, the people you love and the people He put in your path. Time. . .use it wisely.

"Where there is
great love
there are always
miracles."

Willa Cather

Snowy Miracle

Snowy Miracle

Bill Collier

Billy sat atop the wooden fence, watching his nine-year old brother Darren ride the stickhorse that he had made from an old mop handle. He smiled as Darren jerked his horse to make it rear up. Darren whinnied and trotted toward Billy.

"You know what I'll name my horse when I get it?" Darren asked as he hitched his horse to the fence and climbed up beside Billy.

"You're not getting a horse, Darren. Dad told you we don't have space or money for a horse." The two buttoned their jean jackets to ward off the sudden shift of the winter wind. "Besides, I told you that I know what you're getting for Christmas, a Hotwheels Race Track and those race cars you like."

Darren's jaw thrust out with determination. "I want a horse and I want snow for Christmas."

Billy shrugged, feeling sorry for his brother. He had heard Darren's prayers every night for the last three weeks: "Horse and snow. Horse and snow." Springfield, Tennessee had not had snow for Christmas since Darren was three, and the weather report didn't forecast snow, not even sleet.

"It'll take a miracle for Darren's prayers to come true," thought Billy. "C'mon Buddy, I hear Mom calling us, and we haven't gathered the wood for the fireplace yet. The two boys ran to the woodshed.

Snow? Could it be? Darren had awakened in the gray dawn of Christmas, wiping the fog that his breath kept making on his bedroom window. Not satisfied, he ran out the back door. There it was. Snow.

But where was his horse? He ran to one side of the house. Nothing. To the other side. Still nothing. Racing to the front yard, Darren stopped short. There it was. The answer to his prayers was grazing near the edge of the lawn in the lightly, falling snow.

"Mom! Dad! Billy! He's here, and it's snowing!" His family, awakened by Darren's yelling, stood on the front porch awestruck. "Thanks! Oh, thank you! What a great Christmas. Snow and a horse, just like I prayed. I think I'll call him 'Snowy'." He brought the Shetland pony toward them.

"Son. Son, listen to me. We didn't get you this horse. He must have broken loose. Look. The rope end is frayed. Come inside. Let's eat breakfast, and then we'll search the area to find the owner."

Darren held Snowy's bridle, watching him nuzzle the apple Billy offered him. "What a great Christmas. My prayers were answered. I told you it could happen."

Billy nodded in agreement. But to Billy what was really amazing was how Snowy had wandered from Mr. Jensen's farm three-quarters of a mile away; and of all the yards Snowy could have picked, he had picked theirs!

And then the owner, old man Jensen, had said that he didn't want the pony because his kids were grown and gone and he was just too old to care for the pony anymore. So Mr. Jensen struck a deal with his dad. Twenty-five dollars! And firewood. Mr. Jensen would need firewood he said, and he wanted Darren to take good care of the pony. That's all.

Billy shook his head in wonder. That Christmas a miracle had happened at the Collier farm: a Snowy miracle.

"And do not neglect doing
good and sharing;
for with such sacrifices
God is pleased."

Hebrews 13:16

Miss Claudette Agnes

Miss Claudette Agnes

Shirleen Pastor

For as long as Ernie could remember, she had wanted a bicycle. She had borrowed her friends' bikes until their parents had said, "No more sharing! Bicycles are scarce, and no parts are available to replace anything broken." Even though the war was over, everything was still rationed.

"Uncle Sam could make a zillion bikes, but I still wouldn't get one," Ernie complained to her little sister, Gig. "Momma Lily said that all extra money goes to pay your doctor and medicine."

"I'm glad you're getting better from that old Roo-matic Fever. And that stroke. Wow! You couldn't do anything! Maybe months from now when you're back in school, I'll get a bicycle."

Outside the cold November wind made the leaves shiver on the trees. Louisiana was unusually cold in 1945, but the space heater warmed the small room where the two girls sat on their bed, surrounded by books and paper.

Every afternoon after Gig's nap, Ernie had had to play school with Gig while occupying her three-year-old brother. Ernie, the teacher, gave Gig many F's. Because of her stroke, Gig had had to relearn how to talk, to dress herself, and to learn numbers and read. That weekend she wrote a story for Gig about the fun Ernie would have on a shiny red bike.

Gig learned her lessons because without Ernie she had no playmate. Gig could not be exposed to other children. Polio and germs. Those were the things Momma Lily worried about.

Looking at her, you wouldn't know Gig was eight years old. In fact, she was downright puny. And, as a result of her illness, Ernie thought her only pretty feature was her blonde curls dancing on her head when she giggled. Lately Gig giggled often. Her real name was Claudette Agnes. Ernie knew that Gig hated that name; so she said it to make Gig angry.

"Miss Claudette Agnes" could not be upset in any way. "Her heart is too weak to be stressed," Momma Lily warned. So what Gig wanted Gig always got. Everyone treated her like a princess; that is, everyone except Ernie—when no one was looking.

"Maybe Santa will bring you a bike," Gig said, interrupting Ernie's thoughts. Gig still believed in Santa, but Ernie thought she knew better. She had seen Momma Lily sewing Christmas dresses late at night last year—dresses that later became presents under the tree with "from Santa" tags on them.

"Fire! Momma! Gig's on fire!"

"Throw your quilt on her!" Momma Lily screamed as she came running into the room.

Ernie had been awakened by the stench of bright red and yellow flames scorching Gig's body as yellow curls turned to ashes on her head.

Gig had awakened early when Momma Lily had come in to light the heater and had gone back to bed. Quietly Gig had crawled out of bed, had changed into her new pima cotton petticoat, and sat cross-legged in front of the heater. She was playing a game with re-lighted matches. The direction the match would curl would determine where your boyfriend lived.

Then it happened. A match had burned her finger. She dropped it. The forgotten match had quickly burned into her thin petticoat. Paralyzed with fear, Gig sat there unable to move or speak.

Momma Lily ran in, gathered her up, quilt and all, and threw herself and Gig upon the bed.

"Oh, my Lord! Oh, my Lord!" was all Momma Lily kept crying as she lifted Gig in the quilt and raced out to the Foreman home across the street. The Foremans had a car and sometimes, in emergencies, had taken Momma Lily and Gig to the doctor. Now was the biggest emergency Ernie had ever seen.

Time stopped. The house sat quietly, absorbing the smokey stench into its dull wallpaper. On Momma Lily's bed, Ernie sat stunned as she watched over her brother who lay sleeping, unaware of the trauma.

Like a slap, the awful truth struck her. Her sister could die, could be dead already! The only sister she had. The sister who had been suffering all this time. The sister who had been bedridden, who had not been able to play outside. The sister who had no friends. This sister who had looked to her for fun, for learning, for love.

Ernie's brain whirled with fear and prayers at the same time as she cried out, "No bike! If there *is* a Santa Claus, please don't bring me a bike. Please, Santa, please let my sister live!"

"And if there is no Santa, I know there is a Baby Jesus. Please Jesus, bring my sister back to me. I know I don't deserve her, but I'll never ask for a bike again."

And that's just what Baby Jesus did. Right before Christmas, He brought Gig home—all covered with gauze which camouflaged burns that covered her throat, chest, arms and legs. She was the prettiest Christmas gift that Ernie would receive—EVER.

Ernie danced in her Momma Lily and Daddy Charlie present: shiny, very shiny black patent shoes with little straps that buckled across the top. Dancing shoes. Ernie danced and sang Christmas carols for Gig.

She sang fast and twirled, while her new ruffly green dress umbrellaed around her.

Gig giggled, sitting in a kitchen chair and looking like an angel in her matching red dress. She clapped her hands while swinging her shiny, very shiny black patent shoe-covered feet in time to Ernie's song.

"Give and it will be given to you;

good measure,

pressed down,

shaken together,

running over. . .

for by your standard of measure

it will be measured

to you in return."

Luke 6:38

We Hold The Key

Laura Harris Smith

While in another city once
With Christmas just in view,
I met a man with cup in hand,
Who's coat was torn in two.

He needed help; he needed hope;
He needed food and drink;
And as I gave him all I had,
It gave me pause to think.

I told this man of someone past
Who'd helped me one time too;
Who gave to me all that He had
To make my life brand new.

He held my hand and as I spoke,
His eyes filled up with tears.
He saw my heart, how much I cared,
And smiled—his first in years.

I went my way and he went his,
Both with strengthened hearts;
A homeless soul had found a home,
Received a brand new start.

With all His homes in heav'n and earth,
Christ searches for one more.
The irony: we hold the key
That lets Him in the door.

"Do not neglect to show
hospitality to strangers,
for by this
some have entertained angels
without knowing it."

Hebrews 13:2

Camilla

Camilla

David Vaughn

Christmas season brings out the spirit in most of us. There are some, however, who celebrate Christmas throughout the year. Sister Camilla is one of these.

The people of Belleville, Illinois call her a saint. Sister Camilla has received the keys to the city for her charity, and pastors and clergy praise her work. What had motivated this woman forty years ago to dedicate her life to serving others?

Early in her marriage, Sister Camilla had been faced with the hardship of having to work to support herself and two children. Her husband Harlan, an alcoholic, would leave for weeks at a time. Through it all, she had persevered.

Finally a change took place in their lives. Their teenage son, inspired by an evangelist, found his father, brought him home, and bathed him, all the while telling him how Jesus could help him to stop drinking. Harlan believed his son and stayed sober the rest of his life.

Wanting to repay the gifts that God had given them, Sister Camilla and Harlan saw the need to help others in torment. In 1961, they opened a place called "God's Corner." A place that would welcome alcoholics, prostitutes, drifters, and drug addicts.

The death of Harlan in 1986 did not stop Sister Camilla. Sleeping less than five hours a night, her life has been one of total giving. She has refused to buy things for herself for fear that someone less fortunate would need the money. Everyday, including holidays, she has fed between twenty to sixty people. The local authorities and hospital staff have sent teenagers to her. And even though

44

some of the thankless have returned Sister Camilla's kindness by stealing from her and damaging her small home, her spirit has never been broken.

Now eighty-four, Sister Camilla, with her daughter Carol, continues to do odd jobs to support her need to help others. When she is asked why she worships a God that allows such grief and suffering in the world, Sister Camilla Vaughn's face breaks out into a big smile as she explains: "God is my beloved. He is my bright morning star, my rose of Sharon. He is worth more to me than silver, than gold—than diamonds. His love makes me shout with joy."

What a wonderful faith! What a wonderful Christmas heart.

*"People show what they are
by what they do with
what they have."*

Author Unknown

A Christmas Prayer

A Christmas Prayer

Leonard Ahlstrom

Each year, Father Frank, a Jesuit priest, is invited to celebrate Christmas with a family from his congregation. It has always been a joy for him, now in his early seventies, to watch children open their presents with uncontrollable excitement. This one particular year, he recalls, was different. The Anderson family had been going through their most difficult time ever.

Months earlier, the dad had been laid off from a well-paying job due to company downsizing. He had looked relentlessly for work, but had had to settle for odd jobs to pay the bills. Times were hard, especially with the holidays upon them. However, the family had managed to stay in good spirits; in fact, no one would have imagined their struggle just by looking at them.

"Surely I can offer words of encouragement during this Holy season," thought Father Frank as he made his way to their home Christmas Eve.

Cheerful smiles and a cup of hot apple cider greeted him at their door. "Come in, Father Frank," the dad said. "The girls are so excited."

"Merry Christmas, Father. We're glad that you could join us," added his wife. Their two young daughters ran to the door, gave Father Frank a big hug, took his hand, and pulled him hurriedly into the living room. There in the corner stood a beautifully decorated tree, under which were two small presents.

After a simple yet tasty Christmas dinner, everyone gathered near the tree. The mother led the family in their favorite carols. Finally the dad said, "Okay, girls, you can open your presents." The younger daughter immediately jumped up with a shout of delight.

"Wait! Wait!" The older sister's words stopped her. "First we must say a Christmas prayer."

Father Frank smiled and said, "It would be my pleasure." But before he could say another word, the older girl spoke up again.

"Oh, please, Father Frank, let me pray."

"Well, of course," the priest answered.

Clearing her throat, the girl closed her eyes and softly began, "God, thank you for giving us the best Christmas ever." Father Frank was surprised. Peeking at the little girl, then the two lonely presents under the tree, he wondered how this could be their best Christmas ever.

She continued, "God, I know that it's been hard for Mommy and Daddy lately because of money and all, but it's been the best time in some ways too. We've been able to spend more time together as a family. I hear Mommy and Daddy praying together, and even my sister and I aren't fighting as much as we used to. I guess, what I'm trying to say, God, is thank you for my family. And thank you that we love each other. It's a great Christmas."

There were tears. There were kisses and hugs. And, of course, the girls' presents.

After a while, Father Frank said his good-byes and headed back to his home. Pondering along the way, he thought of how he had gone to comfort the family and was, instead, comforted. He thought of how their struggles had pulled the family together. That night he was reminded of a simple truth— "Love conquers all."

"We must not only give
what we have;
we must also
give what we are."

Cardinal Mercia

Cowboy Boots

Cowboy Boots

Shirleen Louviere

In 1969 in Bayou Vista, Louisiana, a bedroom community in the center of the oil industry's blue-collar area, we elementary teachers did not have the training to deal with the "street-wise," often-abused children transferring in from out of state. These maladjusted children were often disruptive and disrespectful.

One twelve-year old boy in my fourth grade reading class of twenty-one boys was my biggest challenge. Chris came to school in filthy, ill-fitting clothes and in need of a bath. His first half-hour in my room was spent establishing territorial rights by shoving, kicking and cursing anyone in his way. My first half-hour was spent trying to establish some semblance of order.

I consulted a fellow fourth grade teacher who taught the honors reading class. Mr. Landry and I decided that until a student learned and used social skills, learning could not take place.

Our plan was to use the Boy's Town method: A student must establish eye contact; repeat the teacher's command or direction; do what is asked quickly without arguing; accept the consequences of his actions. A hard task for most adults, but necessary to be productive in society.

By Thanksgiving most boys had begun to show improvement in behavior, even though progress in reading was slow. Chris, however, remained a problem. Students still moved their desks away from him to avoid his smell as well as his fists and feet. More action on our part was needed.

Having never met Chris's parents, who never answered our calls, nor came for a conference, we decided that Chris would be bathed, his hair would be cut, and he would receive fresh clothing.

Mr. Landry undertook the job of Chris's hygiene and hair. I secured clothes and a special present, cowboy boots, from my church's thrift store. A miracle then occurred that neither the students nor I could believe.

Chris was so proud of his new appearance that he grinned—a lot. When I complimented him for not kicking his schoolmates, he answered, "I don't wanna mess up my boots, and I gotta keep my clothes clean." Mr. Landry gave him an early Christmas present of a cowboy belt and a can of boot polish, which Chris used immediately while sitting at the entrance of the classroom.

The reaction of Chris's fellow classmates was the next miracle. They wanted to see Chris's new belt and boots, they complimented him on his appearance, and they chose to bring their desks near him.

When my supervisor visited my classroom during Christmas week, he was pleased to see the boys' colored, hand-drawn Christmas pictures displayed on the walls, no paper strewn on the floor, and a circle of boys, including Chris, noisily examining an outboard motor and comparing it to the science book illustration.

We all learned from that experience—sometimes all it takes is a little time and care to change a person's heart.

"Do not let kindness
and truth leave you;
Write them down
on the tablet of
your heart

So you will find favor

and good repute

In the sight of God

and man."

Proverbs 3:3&4

"There is no self

in pure love."

Zoe L. Robicheaux

Christmas In April

Christmas in April

Cheryl Harmon

The dream of most girls is to marry a wonderful man, have beautiful children, live in a nice home, and—you know the rest—live happily ever after.

Here in Mount Juliet, Tennessee, I have also had a special dream come true, one that has been in my heart since I was young. When I had first seen my uncle's newly adopted Korean baby girl, deep feelings awakened in me. I knew that one day I, too, would adopt a Korean baby.

When my husband Mike agreed to share my dream, our son and daughter eagerly joined in the plans. Through the adoption agency, we received pictures of Korean children. Reawakened feelings stirred in me when I saw her—a beautiful three-month old with cleft lip and palate. Without hesitation we knew that she had to be ours.

Next, we addressed the medical problem. We applied to the Operation Smile organization, and they agreed to pay for re-constructive surgery. Our prayers were answered when a Nashville plastic surgeon agreed to do the many surgeries needed.

Finally, word came that the baby would be arriving during the Christmas holiday. Eagerly we decorated the house, bought more baby gifts, and waited.

Then things fell apart. Two weeks before we were to fly to Korea, we were notified that the baby had died of Sudden Infant Death Syndrome. We offered up our grief to God, knowing that He would help us.

With a commitment from Operation Smile, we had a blessing waiting for a child with cleft lip and palate. So, we sought after another child with the same condition. Yes, there was one—a two-month old baby girl.

By the time the arrangement for the new baby was made, Christmas had come and gone. However, our Christmas tree remained. For us, it represented our steadfast faith that our dream would be fulfilled. We would just have to pray harder.

On April, 20, 1996 Mike and our teenage daughter flew in from Seoul, Korea with Jasmine. A local television camera crew was there to capture our happiness. What a special April Christmas we had!

Jasmine is now five years old and is in kindergarten. She still has one more surgery scheduled. When I see her eagerness to accept the daily challenge of school and hear her dreams, I recall that April Christmas, when my long-held dream came true—and is still coming true.

You just have to see Jasmine to believe that my dream was worth the wait.

"Let us consider how to stimulate one another to love and good deeds."

Hebrews 10:24

About the Author—

Leonard Ahlstrom is an award-winning songwriter and producer who has had hundreds of songs recorded by various artists over the last twenty years. While a member of recording artist NewSong, he co-wrote sixteen #1 songs for the group. He is currently a staff songwriter with Warner/Chappell and an author for Point to Point in Nashville, Tennessee.

Leonard is an ordained minister through Harvest International Ministries and lives in the Nashville area with his wife, Rebecca, and their three children.

Merry

"The Christmas Shoes"

Written by Leonard Ahlstrom and Eddie Carswell
Produced by Michael Demus for Michael D Productions, Nashville, TN
Engineered and Mixed by Michael Demus
Lead Vocals—Perry Danos
Programming, guitar and keyboards—Michael Demus
Percussion—Jeremy Hundley
Children's Choir—Melody Ahlstrom, Christin Brown, Delany Cusak,
        Sarah Prouty, Zak Vaughn
Boy Solo—Bradley Gwinn